4114

£8. 50

D1587213

BRITISH RAILWAYS STEAM HAULED PASSENGER TRAINS IN THE FIFTIES

Vol. 1

Compiled by
PETER HANDS

DEFIANT PUBLICATIONS
190 Yoxall Road
Shirley
Solihull
West Midlands
B90 3RN.

Printed on behalf of Richard Netherwood Ltd., by Gorenjski tisk P.O., Slovenia

CURRENT STEAM PHOTOGRAPH ALBUMS AVAILABLE
FROM DEFIANT PUBLICATIONS

VOLUME 1
A4 size - Hardback. 100 pages
-180 b/w photographs.
£8.95 + £1.00 postage.
ISBN 0 946857 12 1.

VOLUME 2
A4 size - Hardback. 100 pages
-180 b/w photographs.
£8.95 + £1.00 postage.
ISBN 0 946857 13 X.

VOLUME 3
A4 size - Hardback. 100 pages
-180 b/w photographs.
£9.95 + £1.00 postage.
ISBN 0 946857 16 4.

VOLUME 4
A4 size - Hardback. 100 pages
-180 b/w photographs.
£9.95 + £1.00 postage.
ISBN 0 946857 17 2.

VOLUME 5
A4 size - Hardback. 100 pages
-180 b/w photographs.
£9.95 + £1.00 postage.
ISBN 0 946857 22 9.

VOLUME 6
A4 size - Hardback. 100 pages
-180 b/w photographs.
£9.95 + £1.00 postage.
ISBN 0 946857 23 7.

VOLUME 7
OUT OF
PRINT

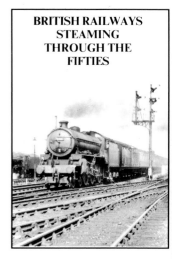

VOLUME 8
OUT OF
PRINT

VOLUME 9
A4 size - Hardback. 96 pages
-177 b/w photographs.
£14.95 + £1.00 postage.
ISBN 0 946857 37 7.

VOLUME 10
A4 size - Hardback. 96 pages
-176 b/w photographs.
£14.95 + £1.00 postage.
ISBN 0 946857 38 5.

VOLUME 1
A4 size - Hardback. 96 pages
-177 b/w photographs.
£14.95 + £1.00 postage.
ISBN 0 946857 39 3.

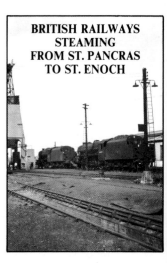

A4 size - Hardback. 96 pages
-173 b/w photographs.
£12.95 + £1.00 postage.
ISBN 0 946857 36 9.

CURRENT STEAM PHOTOGRAPH ALBUMS AVAILABLE
FROM DEFIANT PUBLICATIONS

BRITISH RAILWAYS STEAMING THROUGH THE SIXTIES

VOLUME 11
A4 size - Hardback. 100 pages
-180 b/w photographs.
£10.95 + £1.00 postage.
ISBN 0 946857 24 5.

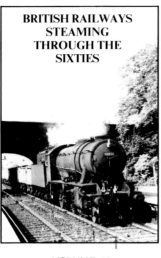

BRITISH RAILWAYS STEAMING THROUGH THE SIXTIES

VOLUME 12
A4 size - Hardback. 100 pages
-182 b/w photographs.
£11.95 + £1.00 postage.
ISBN 0 946857 27 X.

BRITISH RAILWAYS STEAMING THROUGH THE SIXTIES

VOLUME 13
A4 size - Hardback. 100 pages
-182 b/w photographs.
£11.95 + £1.00 postage.
ISBN 0 946857 33 4.

BRITISH RAILWAYS STEAMING THROUGH THE SIXTIES

IN
PREPARATION

VOLUME 14

BRITISH RAILWAYS STEAM HAULED PASSENGER TRAINS IN THE SIXTIES

IN
PREPARATION

VOLUME 1

BRITISH RAILWAYS STEAMING ON THE WESTERN REGION

IN
PREPARATION

VOLUME 4

BRITISH RAILWAYS STEAMING THROUGH CREWE, DONCASTER, EASTLEIGH AND SWINDON

IN
PREPARATION

BRITISH RAILWAYS STEAMING ON THE SOUTHERN REGION

IN
PREPARATION

VOLUME 3

BRITISH RAILWAYS STEAMING ON THE LONDON MIDLAND REGION

VOLUME 3
A4 size - Hardback. 100 pages
-181 b/w photographs.
£11.95 + £1.00 postage.
ISBN 0 946857 28 8.

BRITISH RAILWAYS STEAMING ON THE LONDON MIDLAND REGION

IN
PREPARATION

VOLUME 4

BRITISH RAILWAYS STEAMING ON THE EX-LNER LINES

IN
PREPARATION

VOLUME 3

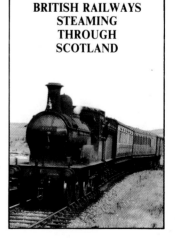

BRITISH RAILWAYS STEAMING THROUGH SCOTLAND

VOLUME 1
A4 size - Hardback. 96 pages
-180 b/w photographs.
£12.95 + £1.00 postage.
ISBN 0 946857 35 0.

ACKNOWLEDGEMENTS

Grateful thanks are extended to the following contributors of photographs not only for their use in this book but for their kind patience and long term loan of negatives/ photographs whilst this book was being compiled.

T.R.AMOS TAMWORTH	W. BOYDEN* BEXHILL	B.W.L.BROOKSBANK LONDON
N.L.BROWNE ALDERSHOT	R.BUTTERFIELD MIRFIELD	R.S.CARPENTER BIRMINGHAM
H.A.CHALKLEY NEWHALL	S.DARTNELL AMINGTON	E.A.ELIAS WOLVERHAMPTON
A.N.H.GLOVER BIRMINGHAM	J.D.GOMERSALL SHEFFIELD	A.E.GOULDING TRURO
D.GOODES LEOMINSTER	PETER HAY HOVE	J.HEAD EASTBOURNE
M.F.HIGSON THE SMOKEBOX	R.W.HINTON GLOUCESTER	F.HORNBY NORTH CHEAM
A.C.INGRAM WISBECH	D.K.JONES MOUNTAIN ASH	BRIAN LESLIE BEACONSFIELD
L.PERRIN BOSTON	A.J.PIKE *	S.PITCHFORTH SANDAL
N.E.PREEDY HUCCLECOTE	B.G.PRICE WOLVERHAMPTON	J.H.PRICE ***
G.W.SHARPE BARNSLEY	JOHN SMITH LENS OF SUTTON	G.WOOD **

*Courtesy of the Frank Hornby collection
** Courtesy of the Mike Wood collection
*** Courtesy of the A.C.Ingram collection

Front Cover - In resplendent external condition LMS *Jubilee* Class 4-6-0 No 45572 *Eire*, from 82E Bristol Barrow Road, heads northwards past Gotherington, near Cheltenham, with an express from Bristol in September 1959. In the background is Bishops Cleeve, the highest point in the Cotswolds. (A.E.Goulding)

ISBN O 946857 39 3

(C) P.B.HANDS 1993
FIRST PUBLISHED 1993

INTRODUCTION

BRITISH RAILWAYS STEAM HAULED PASSENGER TRAINS IN THE FIFTIES - Volume One is a spin-off from the earlier 'Steaming Through The Fifties' albums and adds another dimension to the overall series of books within the 'BR Steaming' range.

The 'BR Steaming' books are designed to give the ordinary, everyday steam photographic enthusiast of the 1950's and 1960's a chance to participate in and give pleasure to others whilst recapturing the twilight days of steam.

Apart from the 1950's and 1960's series, individual albums will be produced from time to time. Wherever possible no famous names will be found, nor will photographs which have been published before be used, but the content and quality of the majority of photographs used will be second to none.

In many respects the 1950's represented the most enjoyable period for post-war steam enthusiasts. Thousands of steam locomotives abounded from Wick to Penzance and with the construction of BR Standard locomotives, the future looked secure for steam on passenger workings for many years to come. The general cleanliness and maintenance of passenger locomotives in the 1950's was far superior to the 1960's, as was the large variety of classes still in service. Who would have envisaged by 1958, with only a handful of main line diesels in service, that within a decade steam hauled passenger trains would be a thing of the past.

BRITISH RAILWAYS STEAM HAULED PASSENGER TRAINS IN THE FIFTIES - Volume One is divided into six chapters, each on a regional basis. For the enthusiast of the individual regions there is a multiplicity of locomotive classes at work on passenger trains, from the humblest tank engine on local duties to the elite engines employed on the crack expresses of the day.

The continuation of the 'BR Steaming' series etc., depends upon you the reader. If you wish to join my direct mailing list for future albums and/or feel you have suitable material of BR steam locomotives between 1948-1968 and wish to contribute them towards this series and other albums, please contact:

Tel. No.
021 745-8421

Peter Hands,
190 Yoxall Road,
Shirley, Solihull,
West Midlands B90 3RN

CONTENTS

CHAPTER ONE - LONDON MIDLAND REGION.

1) The photographer takes advantage of an overbridge to capture this busy lunchtime scene at Watford Junction on 3rd August 1957 where we espy a brace of LMS Stanier Class 5 4-6-0's at work. Approaching is No 45004 (1E Bletchley) on the 12.40pm stopping train from Bletchley. No 45020, also from 1E Bletchley, awaits departure with the 1.20pm local from Euston to Tring. (F.Hornby)

2) The flagship locomotives of the former LMS are the *Coronation* Class Pacifics, employed in the main on the crack expresses to and from London (Euston) and Glasgow (Central). The cream of these expresses is the *Royal Scot.* 66A Polmadie based No 46227 *Duchess of Devonshire* is seen here in action at Hartford on 19th June 1954. (N.E.Preedy)

3) This splendid scene encapsulates the steam era at its height with the inclusion of a locomotive and train, signalbox, array of signals and an engine depot. Class 4P (Compound) 4-4-0 No 41124, from 6G Llandudno Junction, glides serenely beneath the signal gantry as it arrives at Chester (General) on 5th July 1952. (N.E.Preedy)

4) 16A Nottingham based LMS *Jubilee* Class 4-6-0 No 45627 *Sierra Leone* sheds its surplus steam as it approaches Cheadle Heath, near Stockport, with an unidentified express on 26th April 1958. *Sierra Leone* was destined to be one of the last working members of the class being condemned from 8K Bank Hall in September 1966. (R.W.Hinton)

5) LMS Hughes Class 6P5F 'Crab' 2-6-0 No 42707, from 26A Newton Heath, bursts out of Seaton Tunnel with a northbound local passenger train on the former Midland Main Line from St.Pancras - circa 1958. A notice staked in the embankment informs us that Seaton Tunnel is 205 yards long. A brick built hut to the left of 42707 provides shelter for gangers and their like. (A.C.Ingram)

6) Rugby (Midland) is the venue for this photograph of LMS *Royal Scot* Class 4-6-0 No 46140 *The King's Royal Rifle Corps*, allocated to 9A Longsight (Manchester), as it heads an express on an unknown date in 1958. This locomotive ended its working life based at 12A Carlisle (Kingmoor), being condemned in November 1965. (G.W.Sharpe)

7) A rather soiled looking LMS *Jubilee* Class 4-6-0 No 45633 *Aden*, a 10B Preston engine, is in charge of a varied selection of coaching stock whilst in command of a Crewe express at Warrington on 5th June 1954. Preston shed closed in September 1961 after a dreadful fire and as a result *Aden* was transferred to 24L Carnforth. (N.E.Preedy)

8) Cows and wild flowers on the Metropolitan. It's hard to think of this rural scene as part of London Transport until you notice the typical Underground lineside cabling. The Chalfont to Chesham local service, in June 1958, is being worked by former GCR C13 Class 4-4-2T No 67418 (14D Neasden), the coaches of which are vintage 1899. (Peter Hay)

9) The value of smoke deflectors is underlined as exhaust steam enshrouds the top of the boiler and cab of LMS *Coronation* Class 4-6-2 No 46236 *City of Bradford* as it tops up its tender at high speed from Dillicar Troughs, near to Tebay on 5th April 1957. *City of Bradford* is in charge of a Glasgow (Central) - Birmingham (New Street) express. (R.Butterfield)

10) LMS Class 3 2-6-2T No 40118 (9E Trafford Park) travels bunker-first as it rattles a lengthy local passenger train over a metal overbridge near to Heaton Mersey (Stockport) on 29th May 1952. Later in its working life No 40118 had spells at 3E Monument Lane, 8D Widnes and 24L Carnforth before withdrawal in September 1961. (R.W.Hinton)

11) When the BR Standard Classes were introduced in the 1950's they replaced many older engines before they too were ousted by diesel and electric traction. One such Class was the BR Class 4 2-6-4 Tanks. One of their number, No 80038 (lC Watford) has steam to spare as it awaits departure from London (Euston) with a stopping train to Tring in 1954. (A.J.Pike)

12) Lower quadrant semaphores bow their heads to the passing of LMS Hughes Class 6P5F 'Crab' 2-6-0 No 42794, shedded at 41B Sheffield (Grimesthorpe), as it storms the upgrade at Norman's Bridge, Edale with a local passenger bound for Manchester from Sheffield on 4th May 1958. Note the motley collection of carriages, typical of the fifties. (R.W.Hinton)

13) Two bystanders, complete with bicycles, observe the progress of LMS *Coronation* Class 4-6-2 No 46240 *City of Coventry*, a 1B Camden locomotive, as it passes Hillmorton signalbox, Rugby with the shortlived *The Caledonian* express in the Summer of 1958. *City of Coventry* is one of a small number of the class which sported a crest above the nameplate. (N.E.Preedy)

14) A bright, sundrenched summer's day on the West Coast Main Line as LMS *Jubilee* Class 4-6-0 No 45670 *Howard of Effingham*, from 8A Edge Hill (Liverpool), takes refreshment from Whitmore Troughs, between Norton Bridge and Crewe, near to the Staffordshire and Cheshire border, with the down *Empress Voyager* on 9th July 1955. (R.W.Hinton)

15) During the hectic summer months many an engine was pressed into service on heavy holiday expresses. Such is the case with LMS Hughes Class 6P5F 'Crab' 2-6-0 No 42717 (24B Rose Grove) as it steams through Salwick, between Blackpool and Preston, with the 1.05pm Blackpool (Central) to West Hartlepool express on 1st August 1959. (B.W.L.Brooksbank)

16) A frosty and cold winter's day helps to highlight the smoke and steam which is being churned out of former Great Central Railway A5 Class 4-6-2T No 69806, a 39A Gorton engine, seen at Wilbraham Road, Cheadle as it heads a Horwich semi-fast on 26th February 1955. Wilbraham Road, of Great Central vintage, closed in 1958. (R.W.Hinton)

17) We switch from the North of England back to the capital with this next photograph. LMS Class 3 2-6-2T No 40172, allocated to 14B Kentish Town, simmers gently in one of the platforms at St.Pancras with coaching stock on 19th May 1956. Based at Kentish Town for many a year No 40172 was taken out of revenue earning service from there in November 1959. (N.L.Browne)

18) There is no mistaking the location of this picture as we are informed by the wooden station noticeboard that we are at Manchester (Victoria) which is host to a visiting 'Martian'. Black smoke erupts from the chimney as LMS *Jubilee* Class 4-6-0 No 45698 *Mars* (27A Bank Hall) restarts a Newcastle bound express on 14th March 1953. (R.W.Hinton)

19) The next location is at Amersham (London Midland Region/London Transport Executive) where a begrimed LMS Class 5 4-6-0 No 45215, based at 14D Neasden, prepares to leave with the 1.30pm local passenger from Marylebone to Woodford Halse on 19th May 1959. A transfer to 16D Annesley in June 1960 took No 45215 away from Neasden. (B.W.L.Brooksbank)

20) One glance at the horrendous external condition of BR Class 5 4-6-0 No 73074, from 19B Millhouses, suggests this locomotive is overdue for overhaul. If so, it is in the right location as it arrives at Derby on 8th September 1956 with an excursion. To the left of this picture is an unidentified LMS Class 8F 2-8-0. (S.Dartnell)

21) An alert driver looks forward from the cab of his charge as LMS Class 3 2-6-2T No 40053 departs from Chester (General) with a local train - circa 1955. At this stage in time it cannot be ascertained to which depot No 40053 was allocated. Later on in the fifties it was to be found at 1A Willesden and 14B Kentish Town. (R.S.Carpenter)

22) A fine impression of a mighty Pacific in full cry as LMS *Princess* Class 4-6-2 No 46208 *Princess Helena Victoria*, from the shed at 8A Edge Hill (Liverpool), storms through Madeley (closed in 1952), between Stafford and Crewe, with the down *Manxman* on 22nd July 1953. No 46208 was condemned from Edge Hill in October 1962. (R.W.Hinton)

23) The old order at Heaton Mersey (Stockport) on 29th May 1952. LMS Class 3 2-6-2T No 40124, an inmate of the close-at-hand shed at 9F, is in charge of a five coach non-corridor local passenger train. Transferred from Heaton Mersey to 16B Kirkby in February 1961 its life was immediately curtailed by being withdrawn the same month. (N.E.Preedy)

24) As can be seen within this photograph the terrain in and around Warrington is rather flat to say the least. LMS Class 5 4-6-0 No 45259, from 10C Patricroft, steams towards the camera with an express in July 1956. The chequered raised board informs us that there is a facility ahead for the travelling post office, now long extinct. (N.E.Preedy)

25) Another of the mighty LMS *Coronation* Class 4-6-2's is captured on film during the 1950's. No 46225 *Duchess of Gloucester* (5A Crewe - North) is in charge of the northbound *Mid-Day Scot* from Euston to Glasgow on 26th May 1956 a few miles to the north of Crewe. A filled tender suggests that *Duchess of Gloucester* took over this express at Crewe. (N.E.Preedy)

26) Overcast skies and murky looking locomotives add to the gloom at Dudley Port station, between Stafford and Birmingham, on 1st September 1956. The upper quadrant signals a partially clear road ahead of LMS *Jubilee* Class 4-6-0 No 45644 *Howe* (9A Longsight - Manchester), as it heads a down extra. Also present is LMS Class 2 2-6-2T No 41223 (3C Walsall) on a shuttle to Dudley. (F.Hornby)

27) LMS Class 4P 'Compound' 4-4-0 No 41118 (allocation unknown) trundles over Heaton Mersey Bridge (Stockport) with a local passenger commuter train which is bound for St.Pancras from Manchester on 4th April 1953. Records show that No 41118 was at 9A Longsight (Manchester) by January 1957 and at 14B Kentish Town in October 1957. It was withdrawn from 17A Derby in January 1958. (R.W.Hinton)

28) A not too happy driver peers out of his cab towards the photographer on 31st March 1956. His steed, a Fowler designed (equipped with condensing apparatus) LMS Class 3 2-6-2T No 40033, from 14B Kentish Town, waits to leave St.Pancras with empty coaching stock. Five and a half years later and No 40033 was no longer with us being scrapped at Crewe. (N.L.Browne)

29) Transferring northwards several hundred miles we find ourselves at Carlisle (Citadel) once a Roman frontier town. Looking southwards, LMS *Jubilee* Class 4-6-0 No 45600 *Bermuda*, a long-standing 10C Patricroft locomotive, gets an empty stock train on the move on 8th April 1957. *Bermuda* was destined to remain at Patricroft until transferred to 9D Newton Heath in January 1964. (R.Butterfield)

CHAPTER TWO - EASTERN REGION

30) A tranquil scene at Ely in Cambridgeshire in the late 1950's with not one single passenger to be seen. It was this lack of passengers, lured away by the motor car, which was to sound the death knell for many a branch line during the years to come. LMS Ivatt Class 2 2-6-0 No 46465 (31A Cambridge) stands in Ely station with an up local. (A.C.Ingram)

31) Photographs of LNER A3 Class 4-6-2's at Marylebone in the fifties are rare beasts indeed. One of the 'crack' expresses over the former Great Central Main Line, *The South Yorkshireman* is given star treatment in its choice of locomotive. However, its external condition leaves something to be desired. The 'star' is No 60102 *Sir Frederick Banbury*, from 38C Leicester G.C. (R.Butterfield)

32) In a flurry of white smoke a majestically turned out LNER Gresley A4 Class 4-6-2 No 60007 *Sir Nigel Gresley*, from the 'Top Shed' at 34A Kings Cross, emerges from a tunnel at Hadley Wood with the *Centenaries Express* on 11th May 1954. It is hard to believe that almost thirty years has passed since steam power was swept away from this part of the ECML. (D.K.Jones)

33) A 1950's shot of a Railway Correspondence and Travel Society special at Whittlesea, between Peterborough and March. 'The Fensman' is entrusted into the care of 35A New England based LNER B1 Class 4-6-0 No 61391. Although sporting express headlamp discs the locomotive on the left is in charge of a freight train - facing 'wrong line'. (G.W.Sharpe)

34) A busy scene, once the norm, at London's Liverpool Street station in May 1959. Two LNER N7 Class 0-6-2 Tanks pollute the atmosphere with their fumes whilst on duty. To the left of the picture is No 69620 with No 69671 on the right. Both are 30A Stratford engines. By September 1962 steam was to become a memory at Liverpool Street. (N.E.Preedy)

35) LNER A2/3 Class 4-6-2 N0. 60511 *Airborne*, from 52B Heaton, graces the East Coast Main Line at Ranskill with a down express from Kings Cross to Newcastle on 29th May 1958. Ranskill station, situated between Retford and Doncaster, closed during 1958. To the north of the station were the little known water troughs at Scrooby, long since taken up. (R.W.Hinton)

36) Not necessarily an Eastern Region location, but nevertheless worthy of inclusion in this section is LNER Ll Class 2-6-4T No 67740, allocated to 34E New England, seen here near Whitehouse Farm Tunnel with the 4.10pm local passenger train from High Wycombe to Marylebone on 14th September 1957. Between June and October 1958 No 67740 served for a time at 1A Willesden, an unusual location for this type of loco. (Brian Leslie)

23

37) Carrying the headcode of the *Tees-Tyne Pullman* above the front buffer LNER A3 Class 4-6-2 No 60110 *Robert the Devil*, based at 34A Kings Cross, steams through Welwyn North station towards the end of its journey with the heavily laden Pullman cars bound for the capital. No 60110 was later equipped with a double chimney and German style smoke deflectors. (J.Head)

38) A duet of Thompson LNER B1 Class 4-6-0's on show at Nottingham (Victoria) on Saturday 1st August 1959. No 61383 (56F Low Moor) departs with a Poole to Bradford express composed of Southern stock. Sister engine No 61169 (41A Sheffield - Darnall) waits in the station. Both locomotives were withdrawn from service by the end of 1963. (A.C.Ingram)

39) It was not often that locomotives with tenders were employed on services 'facing backwards', but here is one such case. Whatever the reason for this rarity LNER Kl Class 2-6-0 No 61949, from 32A Norwich, waits to depart from Oulton Broad South with a passenger train in 1958. Note the Gresley designed carriage. (A.C.Ingram)

40) An Ivatt LMS Class 4 'Flying Pig' 2-6-0 meanders along in mist-laden countryside at Ecclesfield (Sheffield) in late August 1954. No 43115, a 19A Sheffield (Grimesthorpe) engine, is in charge of a local passenger working. This loco still had some thirteen years of revenue earning service ahead before the inevitable happened - withdrawal in June 1967, from 5D Stoke. (G.W.Sharpe)

41) In steam days Grantham was a stopping point on the East Coast Main Line for expresses to change engines. Its tender filled with coal and water, a spruced up LNER A3 Class 4-6-2 No 60050 *Persimmon,* a local Pacific based at the nearby shed of 35B, restarts a northbound express from Grantham station in 1956 a few years before being fitted with a double chimney and deflectors. (L. Perrin)

42) An immaculate LNER N7 Class 0-6-2T No 69604 (complete with destination board), from 30A Stratford, takes things easy after lifting its heavy train up the bank from Liverpool Street on 30th August 1958. It is seen approaching Bethnal Green station with a down Chingford local. Note the lack of overhead wires above the two tracks in the right of this picture. (B.W.L.Brooksbank)

43) A strong side wind pushes the exhaust steam to one side as LMS Class 5 4-6-0 No 45207, an inhabitant of 56F Low Moor, advances towards a distant signal with *The South Yorkshireman* seen near Barnsley on 14th February 1959. With the distant signal at caution the progress of No 45207 will soon be checked, if not stopped altogether. (D.K.Jones)

44) Looking in ex. works condition Thompson LNER Bl Class 4-6-0 No 61130, from 40B Immingham, is possibly on a running in turn at Peterborough (North) in 1958. With a partially clear road (the signal looking at half-mast) No 61130 sets off from Peterborough station with a Kings Cross to Cleethorpes local passenger, a somewhat lengthy journey for a 'local'. (A.C.Ingram)

45) The far flung location of Norwich, in East Anglia, is the setting for this next photograph. A smartly turned out LNER Ll Class 2-6-4T No 67704, from 32C Lowestoft (Central) clears its cylinder cocks whilst on local passenger duty at Norwich (Thorpe) in September 1953. No 67704 was moved to 30A Stratford from Lowestoft in January 1959 and was condemned from the former in November 1960. (E.A.Elias)

46) The name on the signalbox is Wickford Junction and in May 1956 the possibility that the long branch to Southminster, which it controls, would remain open seemed remote. Electrification and the widening commuter belt became its salvation. The Southend line train blackening the scene is hauled by one of the batch of B12 Class 4-6-0's built to a GER design for the LNER in 1928, No 61576 (31A Cambridge). (Peter Hay)

47) In terms of external condition there is a welcome contrast between this locomotive and the bedraggled condition of the engine in the previous picture. LNER Bl Class 4-6-0 No 61079, a 40B Immingham engine, steams into Wood Green station, some five miles away from Kings Cross, with the 4.10pm express from the London terminus to Cleethorpes on 11th April 1953. (F.Hornby)

48) Safety valves lift from the excess pressure within the boiler of BR *Britannia* Class 4-6-2 No 70041 *Sir John Moore*, a 30A Stratford locomotive, as it prepares for the road within the confines of Liverpool Street station with an eastbound express in 1957. In common with the Southern Region, the Eastern Region also used discs as headcodes instead of lamps on many occasions. (G.W.Sharpe)

49) Specially spruced up for the occasion LNER B12/3 Class 4-6-0 No 61576, a 31A Cambridge engine, after arrival at Colchester station on 30th November 1956. The occasion is the Railway Enthusiasts Club special 'The Suffolk Venturer'. Condemned from Cambridge in January 1959, No 61576 was cut up at Stratford Works three months later. (F.Hornby)

50) A horde of 'spotters' mingle together on the right hand platform as LNER A3 Class traverses 4-6-2 No 60112 *St.Simon*, a locally based engine from 36A, traverses a centre road at Doncaster with an up express bound for Kings Cross on 30th July 1955. The final member of this fine class *St.Simon* was equipped with a double chimney in July 1958 and German smoke deflectors in October 1962. (J.D.Gomersall)

51) The driver stares towards the photographer as his charge steams into Sheffield (Victoria) on a local passenger working in the late fifties. Once of 40B Immingham No 61281 moved on to 40E Colwick (Nottingham) in June 1958. It remained as a faithful servant of Colwick until withdrawn in February 1966. It was scrapped by Birds of Long Marston in July 1966. (G.W.Sharpe)

52) The tranquil countryside scene near Stoke Summit on the East Coast Main Line is disturbed momentarily as an express thunders by. In charge of the train is LNER A2/3 Class 4-6-2 No 60518 *Tehran*, a Newcastle engine based at 52A Gateshead, in the winter of 1958. Moving on to 50A York in June 1960, it was condemned in October 1962. (R.S.Carpenter)

53) An electrification mast lies on the ground to the left of this picture of BR *Britannia* Class 4-6-2 No 70005 *John Milton*, from 30A Stratford, as it departs from Thorpe-le-Soken, the junction for Clacton-on-Sea and Walton-on-Naze, with a departing express circa 1958. In January 1959 *John Milton* moved to pastures new at 32A Norwich. (Peter Hay)

54) Staveley (Central) station, ex. Great Central Railway (closed in 1963), had platforms on the main and Chesterfield Loop Lines, which the 9.24am Chesterfield (Central) to Sheffield (Victoria) local is using. On 6th September 1957 former GCR C13 Class 4-4-2T No 67424 (41A Sheffield Darnall) has a load of three flush panelled LNER carriages. (Peter Hay)

55) A grubby LNER A3 Class 4-6-2 No 60081 *Shotover*, a 50B Leeds (Neville Hill), has a clear road as it accelerates a Newcastle to Kings Cross express towards the flat crossing at Pontop (spelt Pontop Xing on the signalbox nameboard) - circa 1959. Equipped with a double chimney in October 1958, *Shotover* acquired German style deflectors in August 1961. (N.E.Preedy)

56) A busy scene at Bethnal Green station, near to the mighty Great Eastern terminus at Liverpool Street, in the summer of 1954. LNER Bl Class 4-6-0 No 61370, from 30D Southend (Victoria), steams into a platform with an express. Observing the progress of No 61370 is a member of the footplate crew of LNER N7 Class 0-6-2T No 69626 (30A Stratford). (D.Goodes)

57) BR Caprotti Class 5 4-6-0 No 73155, a 41C Millhouses locomotive, coasts along with a summer extra passenger train at Marsh Junction, Grimsby on 9th August 1959. Transferred to 41D Canklow in December 1961, No 73155 cut its links with the Eastern Region after being drafted to the Southern Region (71A Eastleigh) in December 1962. (D.K.Jones)

58) A panoramic view of Peterborough (North) on a misty winter's day in 1958. Steam and smoke issue from LNER A1 Class 4-6-2 No 60124 *Kenilworth* (52A Gateshead) as it storms northwards whilst in charge of a Kings Cross to Doncaster express. LNER N5 Class 0-6-2T No 69276 (34E New England) is on station pilot duties in the background. (A.C.Ingram)

59) Steam trains *underneath* tube trains? Unlikely as it seems, it was a daily scene at Stratford (Low Level) after London Transport's Central Line extension opened in the late 1940's. On a bright, sunny day in July 1956, LNER N7 Class 0-6-2T No 69683, from 30B Hertford East, powers a Palace Gates to North Woolwich local service. No 69683 survived in service at 30B until condemned from there in February 1960. (Peter Hay)

60) Peascliffe Tunnel, to the north of Grantham, a rather lofty and airy structure compared to most tunnels, overlooks the passing of an unidentified express from Kings Cross which has 34A Kings Cross based LNER A4 Class 4-6-2 No 60025 *Falcon* at its head. *Falcon*, was constructed at Doncaster Works during 1937 and originally carried the number 4484. Its single chimney was replaced with a double version in September 1958. (R.W.Hinton)

CHAPTER THREE - NORTH EASTERN REGION

61) Signal gantries with their associated upper quadrant 'pegs' dominate the background of this splendid photograph taken on the approaches to Wakefield (Westgate) station in the early 1950's. Peppercorn inspired, British Railways built, LNER A1 Class 4-6-2 No 60123 *H.A.Ivatt* arrives with a Leeds to Kings Cross express consisting of a mixed bag of carriages, which includes a Gresley car immediately behind the locomotive. (Stuart Pitchforth)

62) I have run out of expletives as to how I can describe the external condition of LMS rebuilt *Patriot* Class 4-6-0 No 45530 *Sir Frank Ree* as it departs from Leeds with an express in the mid-fifties. Obviously the shed staff at 9A Longsight (Manchester) were not concerned with its outward appearance in the eyes of the public. It did however, survive in service until December 1965, being withdrawn from 12A Kingmoor. (G.W.Sharpe)

63) For a brief period between June and September 1958 LMS Class 4 2-6-4T No 42553 was based at 50A York and in July of the same it is employed on a local passenger working near to Monkton Moor. Between September 1958 and condemnation from 51A Darlington in October 1962, No 42553 served from Leeds (Neville Hill), York (again) and Starbeck sheds. It was scrapped at Crewe Works in December 1962. (G.W.Sharpe)

64) Late afternoon shadows extend across the trackwork at the magnificent setting of York station in the summer of 1958. One of the most famous of Sir Nigel Gresley's A4 Class 4-6-2's No 60014 *Silver Link* (34A Kings Cross) steams southwards with the 4.05pm Newcastle to Kings Cross express on 17th August 1958. Think of *Silver Link* and we then think of one of the famous enginemen - Ted Hailstone, a regular driver. (Stuart Pitchforth)

65) Still at York, we turn northwards and to the 'racing ground' between York and Darlington. LNER A3 Class 4-6-2 No 60110 *Robert the Devil* (allocation not known) roars through Pilmoor with an express consisting of a mixed bag of carriages in 1956. This location is roughly halfway between Kings Cross and Edinburgh, some 204 miles from London. (G.W.Sharpe)

66) BR Class 5 4-6-0 No 73160, allocated to 55E Normanton, is seen at work on a holiday extra, N574, in the summer of 1957 or 1958, as it hurries past the camera near to Harrogate. Introduced into service in January 1957 at 52C Blaydon, No 73160 ended its days on the London Midland Region being withdrawn from 9H Patricroft in November 1967. (G.W.Sharpe)

67) A fine panoramic view of Goose Hill Junction, Normanton in May 1959. 52A Gateshead based LNER Al Class 4-6-2 No 60115 *Meg Merrilies* has both footplatemen peering out of the same side of the cab as their charge heads towards the camera. *Meg Merrilies* is in charge of the 11.15 am (Sunday's only) express from Edinburgh - Kings Cross.(Stuart Pitchforth)

68) Until the introduction of more modern motive power the Gresley designed D49 'Hunt' and 'Shire' D49 Class locomotives were often employed on local passenger and semi-fast trains at various locations within the north east. On 17th July 1955 No 62739 *The Badsworth* works a semi-fast at its home base of Scarborough, from whence it was withdrawn in October 1960. (R.Butterfield)

69) Exhaust gases are thrown clear of the boiler and cab of LNER A3 Class 4-6-2 No 60084 *Trigo*, from 50B Leeds (Neville Hill), as it powers the ten coach *North Briton* past Osmondthorpe, a few miles from Leeds on 15th June 1957. A long-standing occupant of Neville Hill, *Trigo* was drafted to 52A Gateshead in December 1963, a final move prior to withdrawal in November 1964. (Stuart Pitchforth)

70) A gloomy day in 1957 helps to darken the interior of York station. An unknown engine simmers in the left of this picture whilst on the right a group of young spotters look, without apparent enthusiasm, at the passing of LNER Al Class 4-6-2 No 60119 *Patrick Stirling* (34A Kings Cross) as it heads northwards with the down *Flying Scotsman*. (Stuart Pitchforth)

71) More Pacific power, this time in the shape of 34F Grantham based LNER A3 Class 4-6-2 No 60048 *Doncaster* as it makes tracks with an express consisting in the main of Gresley coaching stock in March 1959 near Hartlepool. Note the small 'trough deflectors' which were superseded by German style deflectors two months later, possibly after overhaul at Doncaster Works. (N.E.Preedy)

72) Another LNER A3 Class 4-6-2 No 60038 *Firdaussi*, from 52A Gateshead, this time in resplendent external condition, departs from the north end of Wakefield (Westgate) under clear signals with a down express in September 1959. Equipped with a double chimney a month or so earlier, *Firdaussi* was destined never to carry German deflectors. (Stuart Pitchforth)

73) A raised upper quadrant clears a path for LMS Hughes Class 6P5F 'Crab' 2-6-0 No 42704, an inhabitant of 26A Newton Heath (Manchester), as it rids itself of excess boiler pressure at Ripon in the mid-fifties. A favourite of Newton Heath, No 42704 was drafted to 26C Bolton in September 1962, a depot from which it was to die in October 1963. The final rites were performed at Horwich Works a month later. (G.W.Sharpe)

74) A phalanx of signals supported by wires from a gantry help to fill the foreground of this picture taken at Selby on 5th April 1957. LNER D49 Class 4-4-0 No 62761 *The Derwent*, a local inhabitant of the nearby shed at 50C, draws its train, the 12.30pm local passenger from Hull, over the swingbridge and into the station. Eight months later and *The Derwent* was with us no more. (B.W.L.Brooksbank)

75) 34A Kings Cross based LNER A1 Class 4-6-2 No 60149 *Amadis*, built at Doncaster Works in 1949 by British Railways steams past the camera with a Leeds to Kings Cross express on 16th June 1957 at Beeston Junction. Reallocated to 36A Doncaster in October 1958, it was to be its final move being taken out of service from there at the tender age of fifteen - such a waste. (Stuart Pitchforth)

76) Sulphurous fumes, with their associated pieces of soot and clinker (as many a spotter has found out to his cost when leaning out of carriage windows) trail behind LNER A3 Class 4-6-2 No 60048 *Doncaster*, from 36A Doncaster, as it speeds by the camera at Pilmoor with an Edinburgh (Waverley) to Kings Cross express on 8th September 1957. (R Butterfield)

77) More black smoke and fumes as LNER D49 Class 'Shire' 4-4-0 No 62720 *Cambridgeshire*, based at 53B Hull (Botanic Gardens), pollutes the atmosphere as it rattles through Hessle station, on the outskirts of Hull, with an unidentified express in the summer of 1957. The writing was on the wall for *Cambridgeshire* with just two years of service left. Withdrawal came from 53A Hull (Dairycoates) in October 1959. (G. W. Sharpe)

78) London Midland locomotive power invades the scene at York, a bastion of former LNER traction, on an unknown day in 1959. LMS Class 4 2-6-4T No 42174 far from its home ground at 17A Derby, steams southwards through the racecourse station and heads towards Chaloner's Whin Junction with a local passenger. This station, with its host of tracks, was an ideal location for spotters. (G.W Sharpe)

79) LNER A4 Class 4-6-2 No 60025 *Falcon* (34A Kings Cross) speeds beneath an overbridge (a weird looking structure), near Oakenshaw, with the 2.15pm Sunday's Only express from Kings Cross to Edinburgh (Waverley) in May 1959. Oakenshaw station, of Midland Railway origin, situated between Royston and Normanton had closed as early as 1870, presumably on the orders of a Victorian Dr. Beeching! (Stuart Pitchforth)

80) 34A Kings Cross based LNER A3 Class 4-6-2 No 60039 *Sandwich* clatters over trailing points at Beeston Junction, between Leeds and Wakefield, on a warm sunny day on 16th June 1957 with an express consisting in the main of 'blood and custard' coaches. *Sandwich* later acquired a double chimney (July 1959) and German smoke deflectors (June 1961). (Stuart Pitchforth)

81) We return again to the racecourse station at York (Holgate) on 30th August 1952 (presumably a Bank Holiday) where we espy LNER B16/1 Class 4-6-0 No 61458 (50A York) which has been pressed into service on a summer cross-country express as it approaches York station. The two leading coaches are still in varnished teak livery every inch a Gresley design. (Peter Hay)

82) The sight of a double-headed combination of LNER D49 Class 4-4-0's was to become a rarity as the 1950's drew to a close, their duties being taken over by more modern forms of traction. No 62749 *The Cottesmore* (50B Leeds - Neville Hill) and No 62736 *The Bramham Moor* (50D Starbeck) combine their power with an express at Harrogate - circa 1957. (G.W.Sharpe)

83) We take our leave of the North Eastern Region chapter with this photograph of 55C Farnley Junction based LMS Class 5 4-6-0 No 45063 as it passes a raised upper quadrant signal at Monkton Moor with a local passenger consisting of a mixture of coaching stock - circa 1956. Destined to remain at Farnley Junction until March 1964 No 45063 was eventually withdrawn from service in November 1966, from 55A Leeds (Holbeck). (G.W.Sharpe)

CHAPTER FOUR - SCOTTISH REGION

84) Tayport in high summer. The hot sun beats down upon LNER B1 Class 4-6-0 No 61278, a local inhabitant of 62B Dundee Tay Bridge, as it arrives with a passenger train on 17th June 1958. An elderly semaphore clears the path for a passenger train which is setting off in the reverse direction. No 61278 was destined to remain on the books at Tay Bridge shed until both died in April 1967. (F.Hornby)

85) 12A Carlisle (Kingmoor) LMS *Jubilee* Class 4-6-0 No 45691 *Orion* seen at speed near Lockerbie with the empty coaching stock of a mail/passenger train on 13th June 1959. *Orion* is one of a legion of *Jubilee's* allocated to Kingmoor and it did not leave the Carlisle area until July 1962 when it was transferred to 24E Blackpool. (D.K.Jones)

86) Despite the fact that steam suburban workings over the former LNER lines in Glasgow amounted to several hundred every day, photographs of them are not common. Maybe it was because they presented a rather uniform appearance with a Gresley 2-6-2T hauling modern coaches, as opposed to the diversity to be seen on services around Edinburgh. No 67604 (65H Helensburgh) nears Partick Junction on 27th March 1959 with a local. (Peter Hay)

87) The oval window in the door of the coach next to LNER J83 Class 0-6-0T No 68478 (64B Haymarket) can only belong to a Pullman car and is in fact part of the one-time *Mauchline Belle*, by September 1952 just SC218M. The scene is at the west end of Edinburgh (Waverley) station, when these engines did most of the piloting there. (Peter Hay)

88) Railway stations could hardly come in a more basic form than the one seen in this picture. It is Philorth Bridge Halt, on the St.Combs Light Railway from Fraserburgh. As there was no turntable at St.Combs the train is being worked tender-first by LMS Class 2 2-6-0 No 46460 on 5th August 1953, fitted with a cowcatcher at each end as the line was unfenced. The St.Combs branch closed in 1965. (Peter Hay)

89) Arbroath's gas-lit station was the eastern terminus of the local suburban service along the north bank of the Tay, and in April 1958 saw a daily procession of steam hauled trains. Most of them were worked by LNER C16 Class 4-4-2 Tanks like No 67486 (62B Dundee Tay Bridge), here waiting at the west end of Arbroath station ready to return to Dundee (East) on a local passenger. (Peter Hay)

90) Most former North British Railway signalboxes had a hipped roof, like the one shown in this picture of Dunfermline (Upper) at the east end of the station, dating from about 1910. Passing it on 22nd April 1957 is a local working from Thornton Junction headed by LNER 'Glen' D34 Class 4-4-0 No 62475 *Glen Beasdale*, from the depot at Thornton. Note the NBR carriage behind the signalbox. (Peter Hay)

91) It would seem that the fireman on LNER C16 Class 4-4-2T No 67501, from the nearby shed at 61B Ferryhill, has been rather heavy with the shovel while his engine was standing idle, and now it is on the move an unexpected cloud of smoke is the result. This pall is cast over the yard at the south end of Aberdeen station as No 67501 departs with a local on 5th August 1953. (Peter Hay)

92) At one time Edinburgh's local passenger traffic was moved by trams and trains, but buses killed them both. Even DMU traction could not make the North Leith services pay, after they took over from traditional steam trains in 1958. LMS Class 3F 0-6-0 No 57559 (64C Dalry Road), a long-serving Edinburgh engine, waits to leave North Leith for Edinburgh (Waverley) with the 1.43pm service on 7th April 1958. (Peter Hay)

93) The use of 0-6-0 goods engines on suburban passenger trains was not common in Glasgow, though it did seem to happen more on Saturdays when, before the coming of the two day weekend, there was a minor 'rush hour'. 15th April 1959 is a Saturday and LMS Class 3F 0-6-0 No 57607, from 65D Dawsholm, is used on the 12.28pm Rutherglen to Balloch via Glasgow (Central Low Level) seen passing Partick East Junction. (Peter Hay)

94) Enthusiasts specials were not just the preserve of the late fifties or the sixties, but one can go back a lot farther than that. LMS Class 2P 4-4-0 No 40616, a 68C Stranraer locomotive, is employed on a 'Scottish Tour' on 1st June 1950. It is seen here awaiting departure from Castle Douglas station on the now defunct Dumfries to Stranraer route. (A.J.Pike)

95) The antique gas-lamps on the platforms and footbridge are an indication of how little change there had been on many parts of the Scottish Region by April 1958. The most modern items in this photo of a Dundee - Arbroath local service at Broughty Ferry were probably the point rodding, the flush panelled LNER coach coupled to LNER C16 Class 4-4-2T No 67486, and the blue and white BR totem on the lampost. (Peter Hay)

96) As the 9.18am Oban to Glasgow (Buchanan Street) arrives at Killin Junction on 28th March 1959 behind LMS Class 5 4-6-0 No 45119 (65B St.Rollox), passengers from Killin are waiting to join and the crew of LMS Class 2P 0-4-4T No 55195 (63B Stirling) look out for customers for the Killin branch train. Killin Junction sees no travellers now, having closed in 1965. (Peter Hay)

97) A cold 28th March 1959 at Inverkeithing and the solitary passenger is well wrapped up. Travellers from the steam-heated local train from Dunfermline, hauled by LNER 'Glen' D34 Class 4-4-0 No 62478 *Glen Quoich*, from 62A Thornton Junction, who are making the connection into an Aberdeen - Edinburgh service due shortly, hope it is running to time, though they do have a waiting room for shelter. (Peter Hay)

98) Once referred to as 'the last great slumscape of northern Europe', Glasgow's stone-built tenements would have endured for many years, but their inhabitants deserved better accommodation and got it. Amongst the improvements to their lives was the end of smoke from steam engines like LNER J37 Class 0-6-0 No 64581, stopping at Partick Hill with a Saturday train from Springburn to Hyndland, in April 1957. (Peter Hay)

99) In 1953 Glaswegians living near the Cowlairs incline suffered from smoke to an appalling degree from trains, steelworks and the power station. Each train up the bank contributed two lots of smoke, from the train engine - in this case LNER Dll Class 4-4-0 No 62687 *Lord James of Douglas* - and the LNER N15 Class 0-6-2T banking at the rear. (Peter Hay)

100) Introduced into service in 1899 by the Great North of Scotland Railway it is amazing that fifty odd years on examples of these locomotives were still at work on passenger services. D40 Class 4-4-0 No 62269 ambles past the gasworks at Elgin with the five coach 1.00pm service to Lossiemouth on 28th June 1953. No 62269 looks in remarkably fine external condition at this point in time. (R.Butterfield)

101) Thornton Junction was the railway capital of the Kingdom of Fife, at least in the 1950's. Astride the ECML between Edinburgh and Dundee, it was the centre from which lines radiated in all directions to serve the important coalfields, and many carried passenger services. LNER D30 Class 4-4-0 No 62436 *Lord Glenvarloch* waits to return to its base at Dunfermline with a local on 22nd April 1957. (Peter Hay)

102) Before the 'Blue Electrics' came to north Clydeside, suburban services over ex. LNER lines were mostly worked by LNER V1 Class 2-6-2 Tanks like No 67680, from 65A Eastfield (Glasgow). On 30th March 1959 it is seen making a vigorous start from Jordanhill station as it passes Whiteinch East Junction signalbox, where the lines from Maryhill join those from Clydebank. (Peter Hay)

103) Two railwaymen enjoy autumn sunshine as they pass the time of day at Mallaig, between duties, on a bench to the left of this picture. Sizzling gently as it also enjoys the heat of an 'Indian Summer', LNER K2/2 Class 2-6-0 No 61781 *Loch Morar* stands at the head of an express. One of a batch which had the 'luxury' of a side-window cab, *Loch Morar* was to become surplus to requirements in December 1958. (R.Butterfield)

104) When BR Standard classes were introduced in Scotland they replaced many an older engine, but like their counterparts on the rest of the British Railways system their lives were relatively short-lived. BR Class 5 4-6-0 No 73009 leaves Glasgow (Buchanan Street) and heads homewards towards Perth with an express in 1958. Eight years later and No 73009 was no more, condemned from 67A Corkerhill (Glasgow) in July 1966. (R.Butterfield)

105) High summer on the former Glasgow, Paisley and Kilmarnock Joint Railway near Caldwell, between Glasgow and Kilmarnock. A less than clean LMS Class 2P 4-4-0 No 40687, from 67B Hurlford, approaches the camera with a lengthy local passenger on 7th August 1954. Withdrawn from Hurlford in October 1961, No 40687 was placed in store for some two years before being scrapped at Connells, Calder in August 1963. (Peter Hay)

106) The heat of a summer's day reflects off the clean exterior of LNER A2 Class 4-6-2 No 60535 *Hornet's Beauty*, a resident of 64B Haymarket, as it simmers at the head of an express at Perth station on 2nd June 1951. In October 1963 *Hornet's Beauty* was drafted to 'enemy territory' - the LMS - at 66A Polmadie (Glasgow) where it survived until June 1965. (W.Boyden)

107) LMS *Coronation* Class 4-6-2 No 46232 *Duchess of Montrose*, one of a small fleet of this famous class to be allocated to 66A Polmadie (Glasgow), proudly carries the headboard of the short-lived *Caledonian* express as it swings through Rutherglen on the approaches to Glasgow (Central) at the end of its long journey from Euston on 20th July 1958. (N.E.Preedy)

108) Despite the fact it is summertime a sea mist hangs over the landscape at Nigg Bay. LNER A2 Class 4-6-2 No 60525 *A.H.Peppercorn*, from 61B Aberdeen (Ferryhill), pounds by the camera with the *Aberdonian* (bereft of headboard) on 27th June 1955. Named after its auspicious designer, *A.H.Peppercorn* was introduced into traffic during 1947 and served all of its life at Ferryhill until condemned in March 1963. (R.Butterfield)

109) On the north side of the Clyde, west of the centre of Glasgow, the lines of the former LMS and LNER wove in and out of one another in their attempts to capture as much traffic as possible, and this accounts for the multiplicity of tracks here at Kelvinhaugh. LNER V3 Class 2-6-2T No 67614 (65H Helenburgh) is on a Saturday morning commuter train to Glasgow Queen Street (Low Level) on 27th March 1959. (Peter Hay)

110) LNER A3 Class 4-6-2 No 60097 *Humorist*, from 64B Haymarket, stands at Dundee with an express in 1956. This locomotive, constructed at Doncaster Works in 1959, was unique with regards to the style of smoke deflector with which it was equipped and it was destined never to carry the German style of the same. It departed from the famous Haymarket shed in December 1961, for nearby 64A St.Margarets. (R.W.Hinton)

111) With the River Tay widening as it neared the end of its journey to the Firth and the open sea from the Highlands it was necessary for a lengthy bridge to be constructed to help connect the towns of Perth and Dundee. A female pedestrian observes the progress of LMS Class 5 4-6-0 No 44718 (60A Inverness) as it navigates the single track structure with an express for Dundee on 18th May 1959. (D.K.Jones)

112) The former NBR C15 Class 4-4-2 Tanks were built by the Yorkshire Engine Co., and known as 'Yorkies'. The last two finished their lives based at 65A Eastfield (Glasgow) and worked the Craigendoran - Arrochar push-pull service. Here No 67460 comes through lush vegetation of the lower end of the West Highland line near Faslane with a southbound trip from Arrochar in September 1959. (Peter Hay)

113) Ahead of LNER D30 Class 4-4-0 No 62418 *The Pirate* is a forest of upper and lower quadrant signals, as it crosses the ECML at Thornton Junction, controlled by two signalboxes: Junction station (left) and Junction Central (in the distance). The train is heading towards the colliery tip on the right, round the base of which runs the Fife Coast line, with the 12.08pm to Crail on 22nd April 1957. (Peter Hay)

114) We take our leave of Scotland by moving from the flatlands of Fife to the Highlands at Boat of Garten on 19th June 1958. The two coach train in the left of the island platform is from Craigellachie. In the distance is a Highland Section train from Forres to Aviemore hauled by an unidentified LMS Class 5 4-6-0. Closed in 1965 by BR, Boat of Garten station is now part of the preserved Strathspey Railway. (F.Hornby)

115) With a water tank and twin upper semaphores in attendance former LSWR Adams 02 Class 0-4-4T No 24 *Calbourne* (70H Ryde) prepares to leave Ryde Pier station with a passenger train - circa 1959. The island system was decimated in the fifties and sixties, but today we can still travel from Ryde Pier to Shanklin, albeit by electric power and we can still ride behind *Calbourne* from its preserved base at Haven Street. (M.F.Higson)

116) Enthusiasm and enthusiasts at Portsmouth on 3rd May 1953 as LBSC 'Brighton Atlantic' 4-4-2 No 32425 *Trevose Head*, from 75A Brighton, arrives with a Stephenson Locomotive Society special. The origins of the 4-4-2 wheel arrangement were in America (1879) and a number were built for the Atlantic Coast Line (1894), hence the name of 'Atlantic'. (D.K.Jones)

117) An almost deserted scene at Ashford on 3rd April 1954. Dollops of white smoke cascade from the funnel of unrebuilt SR *Merchant Navy* Class 4-6-2 No 35028 *Clan Line*, complete with regalia, as it speeds through the station with the *Golden Arrow*. Constructed in December 1948 *Clan Line* was rebuilt at Eastleigh Works in October 1959 and preserved after withdrawal from 70A Nine Elms in July 1967. (G.Wood)

118) The original platform has been extended by wooden planking at Charing Cross, in the heart of London, where we espy SR *Schools* Class 4-4-0 No 30926 *Repton*, a 73B Bricklayers Arms locomotive, at the head of the 10.25am express to Hastings on 20th April 1957. Withdrawn from 70D Basingstoke in December 1962 *Repton* was preserved (cosmetically) in America, but has since returned home for active restoration. (B.W.L.Brooksbank)

119) A lone spotter occupies a platform at Tunbridge Wells West as a raised upper quadrant clears the way for the departure of SR Q Class 0-6-0 No 30534, from 75C Norwood Junction, on 23rd July 1953. A longstanding inmate of Norwood Junction, No 30534 moved on to pastures new at 75A Brighton in April 1961. A final move to 75D Stewarts Lane in November 1962 was a prelude to withdrawal the following month. (D.K.Jones)

120) This delightful setting is at Instow where whitewashed dwellings look down upon the small station. A white plume of steam flows from the safety valves of SR M7 Class 0-4-4T No 30251, from 72E Barnstaple, as it waits patiently with the 4.21pm Exeter to Torrington local passenger train on 19th May 1956. Instow station closed during 1965, lasting a little longer than No 30251, which was condemned in 1963. (N.E.Preedy)

121) Coal in Kent had close associations with railways. It was first found whilst digging during an early attempt at a Channel tunnel on the foreshore near Dover, and at one time there were nearly a dozen collieries at work. The upside down mine tubs on the left of this picture belong to Snowdown Colliery. SR Dl Class 4-4-0 No 31509 (73E Faversham) arrives at Snowdown Halt on 6th September 1958. (Peter Hay)

122) From nationalisation in 1948 until the closure of the bulk of the former Somerset & Dorest Railway in 1966, it was owned by the London Midland, Southern and Western Regions of British Railways. The Southern Region managed its operations from 1950-1958. On 12th March 1955 LMS (SDJR) Class 4F 0-6-0 No 44560 (71G Bath Green Park) waits in Templecombe west yard with the ECS of a stopping train to Bath. (F.Hornby)

123) The West Country was dominated by the Western Region, but there were enclaves of Southern Region territory intermixed, mainly in North Devon and North Cornwall. One of the Southern outposts was at Bodmin, closed during 1967. On 17th August 1959 steam was still in command on local passenger workings. SR 02 Class 0-4-4T No 30236, from 72F Wadebridge, is at Bodmin with a three coach train bound for Wadebridge. (Peter Hay)

124) Colour light signals dominate the background at London Bridge station on 30th April 1950. Rebuilt *West Country* Class 4-6-2 No 34016 *Bodmin* (74B Ramsgate) threads its way through the maze of third rail electrified lines and steams to a halt with the 3.25pm Margate - Deal - Charing Cross express. Withdrawn from 70D Eastleigh in June 1964, *Bodmin* has been restored to life at the Mid-Hants Railway. (B.W.L.Brooksbank)

125) Despite the live third rails steam still holds its head high on a damp day on 31st May 1958 at Earlsfield in London, between Clapham Junction and Wimbledon. SR *Lord Nelson* Class 4-6-0 No 30855 *Robert Blake*, allocated to 71A Eastleigh, storms through with an express. With the surface of the platform apparently breaking up and the presence of weeds, there was an air of dereliction about the place at this stage in time. (N.L.Browne)

126) The small station looks prim and proper at Blackwater, on the Isle of Wight, on a crisp and cold winter's day in 1955. SR 02 Class 0-4-4T No 32 *Bonchurch* (71E Newport) rattles its antiquated carriages over the level crossing on the approach to the station. Blackwater station, centre of a system that ran from Newport to Sandown and Ventnor Town, closed in 1956. (D.K.Jones)

127) Although the sunshine is bright, the white exhaust from SR L Class 4-4-0 No 31766, from 73E Faversham, is blown sideways by a strong autumn wind. Seen at Malling, near Lewes, No 31766 heads its lightweight train, the 10.55am Brighton to Tonbridge on 5th October 1956. Ousted by electrification in June 1959, No 31766 was transferred to 70A Nine Elms, from where its last fire was drawn in February 1961. (Peter Hay)

128) This relatively busy scene at Fareham station on 18th May 1955 belies the fact that the lines in the right of this picture to Gosport had ceased to carry passengers for some two years. A railwayman in the left of the frame totally ignores the passing of SR U Class 2-6-0 No 31637 (70F Fratton) as it sweeps round the tight curve as it arrives at Fareham with a Portsmouth to Eastleigh train. (N.L.Browne)

129) Another outpost of the Southern Region was at Camelford, between Launceston and Wadebridge in North Cornwall. The station nameboard announces 'change for Boscastle and Tintagel' though neither could be reached by rail - presumably there was a bus service to these destinations. SR 'Greyhound' T9 Class 4-4-0 No 30711, of 72A Exmouth Junction, stands in the station with a passenger train on 23rd May 1956. (N.E.Preedy)

130) Judging by the state of the wooden fences the station at Templecombe (Upper) had seen better days. 72A Exmouth Junction based SR rebuilt *Merchant Navy* Class 4-6-2 No 35009 *Shaw Savill* stands in the station with an up express bound for Waterloo - circa 1959. Templecombe (Upper) on the line between Salisbury and Yeovil demised in 1966, two years after *Shaw Savill* had been withdrawn from Exmouth Junction. (A.C.Ingram)

131) Though recognised as the busiest railway complex in the world, Clapham Junction is all but deserted as the photographer clicks his shutter to record the passing of a solitary train on 2nd April 1958. SR *Schools* Class 4-4-0 No 30903 *Charterhouse* (70A Nine Elms) passes a block of grim tenement buildings as it heads westwards with the stock of a down empty stock train. (B.W.L.Brooksbank)

132) Eastleigh, on the former London and South Western main line from Waterloo, is the setting for this photograph in April 1953. Steaming into view is SR M7 Class 0-4-4T No 30032, an inhabitant of the local shed of 71A, with a local from Southampton to Andover, complete with a set of LSWR carriages. To the left of the picture is SR L1 Class 4-4-0 No 31787 (allocation unknown). (Peter Hay)

133) Summertime on the Sussex Downs. The peace and tranquillity of the countryside is disturbed momentarily by the passing of SR D1 Class 4-4-0 No 31492 (74D Tonbridge) near to Lewes in June 1957 with a Tonbridge line passenger train. The D1 locomotives were a Maunsell rebuild of the earlier Wainwright SEC D Class. No 31492 was taken out of traffic from Tonbridge shed in January 1960 and scrapped at Ashford Works. (Peter Hay)

134) A water column towers over BR Class 4 2-6-4T No 80016, from 75A Brighton and in superb external condition, as it awaits departure from a wet East Grinstead (High Level) station with the 2.25pm passenger to London (Victoria) on 16th March 1957. For many years in the late fifties and early sixties No 80016 was allocated to 75F Tunbridge Wells. (F.Hornby)

135) The gradient board in the right foreground informs us that the track will be sloping downhill at 1 in 100 through Whitstable station. A second photographer (left foreground) also records the passing of BR Class 5 4-6-0 No 73081 (73A Stewarts Lane) as it powers the 9.35am Victoria to Ramsgate express on Monday 5th August 1957. No 73081 was later named *Excalibur* (once carried by *King Arthur* Class 4-6-0 No 30736). (F.Hornby)

136) A Tattenham Corner Royal Train on 5th June 1957. The four coach Pullman carriages, with 'Isle of Thanet' (formerly 'Princess Elizabeth' of 1928) is leading the quartet which houses the Duke of Edinburgh and his entourage which is being hauled by SR *Schools* Class 4-4-0 No 30939 *Leatherhead*, from 73B Bricklayers Arms, in pristine condition with the appropriate Royal Train headcode. (Peter Hay)

137) A 'foreigner in the camp' in April 1957. Basingstoke station hosts an outsider from the Western Region in the shape of GWR *Modified Hall* Class 4-6-0 No 7906 *Fron Hall*, from 81D Reading, which is in charge of a local passenger. In the adjacent platform, to even the balance is SR *Schools* Class 4-4-0 No 30906 *Sherborne*, a 70A Nine Elms locomotive. The wet conditions make life miserable for rail travellers and photographers alike. (D.K.Jones)

138) Paddock Wood station is mainly to the right of this picture and carries the former South East and Chatham main lines from Ashford to Tonbridge. In a more secluded part of the station is SR H Class 0-4-4T No 31005, a 74A Ashford engine, the driver of which is looking towards the camera as he waits with his charge on a local passenger working on 7th June 1958. (D.K.Jones)

139) Another footplateman looks towards the camera from the cab of his steed. SR *Schools* Class 4-4-0 No 30927 *Clifton*, from 73B Bricklayers Arms, has just emerged from the gloom of the tunnel at Folkestone Warren with a down express on 7th August 1952. Faithful to Bricklayers Arms shed for many a year it was drafted to 70B Feltham in January 1961 for one month before moving on to 70A Nine Elms, its last home. (R.W.Hinton)

140) In stark contrast to the external condition of *Clifton* in the previous picture SR Dl Class 4-4-0 No 31494 (73E Faversham) is unkempt and filthy. Passengers crowd the platform at Canterbury (East) - circa 1957, and a young father attempts to bring to the attention of his young child the arrival of the 'Iron Horse'. Before his child was much older No 31494 was with us no more - condemned in August 1960. (D.K.Jones)

141) As old engines fitted for push and pull working became scarce, other types were used that had to run round the coaching stock at each end of the journey. This train from Horsham, leaving Hove in April 1956, is hauled bunker-first by SR E4 Class 0-6-2T No 32562, a 75A Brighton inmate, which is coupled to an LBSCR driving trailer, with an SECR composite at the rear of the train. (Peter Hay)

142) The headcode announces that this train entering Fareham will terminate at Portsmouth & Southsea. It is in fact the 4.08pm from Brockenhurst, worked as usual in April 1955 by SR T9 Class 4-4-0 No 30283 (71A Eastleigh) and five coach set No 837, the first dating from 1899 and the latter from half a century later. The writing was on the wall for No 30283 with withdrawal looming in December 1957. (Peter Hay)

143) A soaking wet and damp Sunday 30th December 1956 assists in keeping steam within the confines of London Bridge (Low Level) station. The steam is issuing from the safety valves of 73B Bricklayers Arms SR E4 Class 0-6-2T No 32472 at the rear of some rather more than ancient coaching stock. The two gentlemen who can be seen are wearing the fashion of the day - long 'Harry Lime' - 'Third Man' macks. (J.H.Price)

144) Lush vegetation overlooks Parkstone (for Sandbanks) station - circa 1955, between Bournemouth and Poole on the former London and South Western main line from Waterloo to Weymouth. Taking advantage of a lofty height the photographer captures on camera the simple lines of SR Q Class 0-6-0 No 30539, from 71B Bournemouth, as it powers a local passenger. (John Smith)

145) This final sequence brings to an end our association with the Southern Region in this book. Southampton Terminus station appears to be devoid of passengers as SR M7 Class 0-4-4T No 30376, of 71A Eastleigh shed, arrives with a local working from Winchester City in 1958. Southampton Terminus (often referred to as Southampton Town) closed to passengers in 1966. (A.C.Ingram)

CHAPTER SIX - WESTERN REGION

146) There is a haze hanging over the City of Bristol where residents of the terraced houses to the right of this picture have optimistically hung their washing out to dry on a wintry 17th February 1958. An immaculate looking GWR *County* Class 4-6-0 No 1003 *County of Wilts*, from 84G Shrewsbury, passes Stapleton Road with a lengthy Plymouth (North Road) to Liverpool (Lime Street) express (reporting number 208). (T.R.Amos)

147) The railways to the west of Swansea were often neglected by photographers, probably because they were off the beaten track and were time consuming places to travel to and from. A major outpost in West Wales is at Carmarthen where GWR 4300 Class 2-6-0 No 6377, housed at the nearby depot 87G, is captured on film in June 1959 with an express. (D.K.Jones)

148) Apart from the advent of diesel traction and Inter-City 125's not a great deal has changed with the infrastructure of Paddington since steam days. The preserved GWR record breaker 'City' Class 4-4-0 No 3440 *City of Truro* visits the mighty terminus on 23rd July 1958 with empty stock. Withdrawn in 1931 it was restored for special workings in the late fifties and withdrawn again in May 1961. (B.W.L.Brooksbank)

149) On the 18th August 1959, GWR 4500 Class 2-6-2T No 4559 (83E St.Blazey) trundles down the Looe branch with a load of holidaymakers bound for the seaside. Despite eleven years of nationalisation, somehow some of the ex. GWR coaches managed to become painted in the old chocolate and cream livery, and appear on local trains like this one which is nearing Sandplace. (Peter Hay)

150) GWR Collett *Manor* Class 4-6-0 No 7824 *Iford Manor* (built at Swindon in 1950), from 83D Laira (Plymouth), pilots GWR *Hall* Class 4-6-0 No 5913 *Rushton Hall* (built at Swindon in 1931), allocation not known, on the final leg of the 1 in 44 climb to Dainton Tunnel with a train of holidaymakers bound for the South Devon resorts from Newport and Cardiff on 22nd August 1953. (A.N.H.Glover)

151) Sporting train reporting number 204, a filthy GWR *Hall* Class 4-6-0 No 4919 *Donnington Hall*, from 81A Old Oak Common, leaves a trail of black smoke as it blasts through Maidenhead with an express on Thursday 26th March 1959. *Donnington Hall* was destined to remain on Old Oak Common's books until September 1962 (avoiding the mass withdrawals of that particular month), moving on to 81F Oxford. (A.C.Ingram)

152) A lovely, warm looking summer's day in the early 1950's. The lower quadrant in the background clears the way for the passing of GWR *Castle* Class 4-6-0 No 7034 *Ince Castle*, an inmate of 82A Bristol (Bath Road), as it rounds the bend at Bayston Hill on the run down to Shrewsbury with an express from Hereford and the south-west. *Ince Castle* was later equipped with a double chimney in December 1959. (H.A.Chalkley)

153) GWR *County* Class 4-6-0 No 1004 *County of Somerset* (83G Penzance) leans to a curve on the approaches to Brent station with an express in August 1951. *County of Somerset*, in common with all of the members of the class was modified with a double chimney, in April 1957. Brent station, not far from the summit of Rattery Bank, closed completely during 1964. (D.K.Jones)

154) The splendour of the magnificent achievements of the civil engineers to create Sonning cutting is clear for all to see in this panoramic view as taken during 1959. GWR *Castle* Class 4-6-0 No 5046 *Earl Cawdor* (84A Wolverhampton - Stafford Road) looks in ex. works condition as it approaches the camera with an express consisting of a mixed bag of stock. Note the unusual position of the distant signal to the left of the frame. (D.K.Jones)

155) A siding, point rodding and disused wooden sleepers dominate the right foreground of this picture. BR Class 4 4-6-0 No 75005, an 89A Oswestry engine, departs from Dovey Junction (Cambrian Section) with a six coach load which forms the 7.55am Shrewsbury to Aberystwyth stopping train on 17th July 1958. A double chimney was fitted to No 75005 in January 1962. (F.Hornby)

156) Pembroke Dock is another outpost of British Railways being a terminus station many a long mile from Whitland, Carmarthen and normal civilisation. A few passengers linger on the platform as GWR 4500 Class 2-6-2T No 5520, from 87H Neyland, combines with an unidentified 2251 Class 0-6-0 to power a local passenger train in June 1959. No 5520 was to die at Neyland shed after withdrawal in September 1962. (D.K.Jones)

157) Despite it being high summer there are only a few passengers to be seen on the platform as a westbound express draws into Newton Abbot station on 22nd August 1953. GWR *Hall* Class 4-6-0 No 4920 *Dumbleton Hall*, sporting a broken 83B Taunton shedplate, pilots GWR *Modified Hall* Class 4-6-0 No 7925 *Westol Hall*, prior to them setting off from Newton Abbot and for the grades on the journey to Plymouth. (N.L.Browne)

158) Purists might argue that this photograph taken at Launton, on the Oxford to Bletchley line should not be included in this chapter. As Launton is only a stone's throw from Bicester it was decided to publish it. LNER K3 Class 2-6-0 No 61886, from 31B March, is about to traverse the level crossing as it arrives at Launton with a Cambridge to Oxford local passenger on 13th August 1959. (N.E.Preedy)

159) Twyford, thirty-one miles from Paddington, between Maidenhead and Reading, is the setting for this next print. Early spring sunshine beats down upon GWR *Modified Hall* Class 4-6-0 No 7917 *North Aston Hall*, (allocation not known), as it speeds along amidst quadruped track with an express on 8th April 1953. During the late fifties and until February 1963 *North Aston Hall* was based at 82D Westbury. (D.K.Jones)

160) During steam days there were many locations which drew spotters in their hundreds and Bristol (Temple Meads) was one such place, with the added attraction of Bath Road shed being within 'sprinting' distance for the brave amongst us. For a brief period BR Class 3 2-6-2T No 82003 was allocated to Bath Road shed (March-August 1958) and it is noted at Temple Meads on a local passenger in July of this year. (G.W.Sharpe)

161) The GWR Collett 5600 Class 0-6-2 Tanks were somewhat of a rarity being employed on local passenger trains on the bulk of the Western Region in England, but in Wales it was a different story entirely, especially in the valleys. Newly allocated to 87F Llanelly, No 5657 waits for passengers at Port Talbot station on 12th December 1959. Note the presence of the unidentified GWR diesel railcar. (D.K.Jones)

162) Swindon was the 'creme-de-la-creme' as far as Great Western fans were concerned with its magnificent workshops and locomotive shed. Sadly, little remains of either today and the workforce of this railway town has had to adopt new skills or move away from the town to find other work. On a miserable 27th July 1958 GWR *Grange* Class 4-6-0 No 6830 *Buckenhill Grange* speeds by with an up express. (N.L.Browne)

163) The delightful stone building at Loddiswell Halt, on the Brent to Kingsbridge branch, closed in 1963, was provided with an outsize platform awning. Not only does it provide shelter to passengers, it also supports hanging pots for plants. With oil lamps and GWR notices on view, GWR 4500 Class 2-6-2T No 5558 (83A Newton Abbot) and its train complete this classic branch line scene on 19th August 1959. (Peter Hay)

164) Patchway, on the outskirts of Bristol, is on the approaches to the mighty Severn Tunnel and this is where GWR *Hall* Class 4-6-0 No 5996 *Mytton Hall*, from 81A Old Oak Common, was to be found on a summer's day in 1954 at the head of a passenger train. The filled tender informs us that *Mytton Hall* is at the beginning of its journey. *Mytton Hall* ended its working life at 84B Oxley being condemned in August 1962. (D.K.Jones)

165) Until the fall of Dr. Beeching's axe the valleys of Wales were a mass of branch lines both for passenger and mineral traffic. Amidst this maze is Coryton Halt (Cardiff Railway) a pleasant rural setting with its single platform. Few passengers are to be seen at this terminus on 21st May 1955 where GWR 6400 Class 0-6-0PT No 6416, an 88A Cardiff (Cathays) engine waits to push its two coach train back to Cardiff. (N.L.Browne)

166) 83A Newton Abbot based BR *Britannia* Class 4-6-2 No 70022 *Tornado* looks in superb condition as it blows off steam at Teignmouth station on 22nd August 1953. *Tornado* is in charge of the 12.30pm Paignton to Manchester express. *Tornado* has handrails on the deflector plates in common with all of the Western Region based *Britannia's*. These were replaced later with hand grips. (N.L.Browne)

167) Cowley Bridge Junction, Exeter was a very pleasant location for the signalmen who worked in this box with the river Exe burbling along nearby. The pioneer GWR Churchward 4700 Class 2-8-0 No 4700, from 81A Old Oak Common, rattles over the connection which leads to Barnstaple and beyond as it sweeps towards Exeter station with a down express filled with holidaymakers on 1st August 1959. (D.K.Jones)

168) Wolverhampton (Low Level) in the autumn of 1956. GWR *Castle* Class 4-6-0 No 7005 *Lamphey Castle* (85A Worcester) draws its lengthy local passenger train from Worcester into this once busy main line station (closed to passenger traffic in 1972). In August 1957 No 7005 was renamed *Sir Edward Elgar* to commemorate the distinguished music composer who was Worcester's favourite son. (B.G.Price)

169) During steam days it was not uncommon to see former LNER locomotives on Western Region territory at locations like this one at Beaconsfield, which was once jointly run by the Great Western and the Great Central. With its grubby stock in tow a less than clean LNER Ll Class 2-6-4T No 67752, of 14D Neasden, draws its Marylebone bound local passenger (the first coach is of GC origin) into the station in 1958. (Brian Leslie)

170) As a main line train calls at the other side of the platform, GWR 4500 Class 2-6-2T No 5572, from 83D Laira (Plymouth), waits patiently for any passengers going down the branch to Fowey on 17th August 1959. The scene is at Lostwithiel, where palm trees on the platform were a speciality. Are they still there? No 5572 still is, saved for posterity by the preservation movement. (Peter Hay)

171) Two GWR *Modified Hall* Class 4-6-0's steam and sizzle side by side on down expresses at Paddington on 19th March 1955. In the left of the picture is No 7924 *Thornycroft Hall* and on the right is No 7900 *Saint Peter's Hall* which is in charge of the 12.30pm to Weymouth. 7924 is from 82D Westbury and 7900 from 81F Oxford. To complete the picture GWR 6100 Class 2-6-2T No 6167 (81B Slough) is also present. (F.Hornby)

172) The spacious platforms at Great Malvern are extremely well maintained by the station staff and the fire buckets are to be seen in their proper place looking like a regimental line-up as GWR 5100 Class 2-6-2T No 4142 (85A Worcester) arrives with a Worcester to Hereford local in 1958. No 4142 had been allocated to Worcester shed during March of this year, having previously been based at 84H Wellington. (A.C.Ingram)

173) Double-heading of steam locomotives were a common sight on heavy passenger and freight workings alike, but this combination is somewhat of a rarity to say the least. White, fluffy clouds provide a backdrop to this picture of BR *Britannia* Class 4-6-2 No 70022 *Tornado* (83A Newton Abbot) as it pilots an unidentified 4300 Class 2-6-0 past the golf course near Shrewsbury with an express from the south west - circa 1955. (H.A.Chalkley)

174) This portrait brings to an end this first album on 'BR Steam Hauled Passenger Trains In The Fifties'. GWR 4500 Class 2-6-2T No 4536, from 82D Westbury, waits at Bristol (Temple Meads) station with a local on 14th June 1956. No 4536 was to fall victim to early withdrawal, being condemned from Westbury shed in April 1959. Scrapping took place at Swindon Works during the same month. (N.E.Preedy)